The Midas Effect

Transforming dreams into reality

Raja Oellinger-Guptara

(serendii)

ISBN 978-3-9503713-3-8

©2014 Copyright by Raja Öllinger-Guptara & serendii publishing

Publisher: serendii publishing, Austria
DREAMICON VALLEY

Table of content

- What You Should Know 10
- No Success Without a Coach. 12
- Flumina de ventre eius fluent aquae vivae. 15
- The Butterfly Effect on Dreams 16
- The Butterfly Does Not See the Hurricane Coming . .21
- Homeless in India. 26
- If You Will It, It Is No Dream .28
- 3Ds. 30
- The Domino Effect 32
- A Nobody in Austria 35
- Ask, Pursue, Agere 37
- HHH or Redwood Principle 40
- Heart = Faith 42
- Begin It!. 44
- The Lever Principle. 47
- Newton's 3rd Law. 48
- 2000 Years Became Reality 50
- Clueless in America 53
- VAT. 55
- KISS 58
- Decision & Commitment 60
- 7-Step Mantra. 61
- The Tipping Point 65
- Multiplier Effect 70
- When Good Becomes the Enemy of the Better. 73
- Outlier Effect. 76
- Metamorphosis 78

- Metamorphosis contra Agere 81
- The moment that Changes Everything 84
- When the Active Displaces the Passive............88
- 30 Seconds to Decide Everything 95
- Act as if 98
- A Nobody Again in Austria.....................100
- HHH Instead of "Burning Your Tires" 102
- The Secret of Repetition 106
- Resistance of Belief 110
- Pavlov Effect 112
- Dream Autopilot..............................114
- Chaos Theory 117
- Renaissance 3.0 119
- Starting Over Three Times.....................124
- The missing link 125

What you should know when reading this book

This book is for those who dare to follow their dreams!

One reason that I have become interested in dreams and that moved me to write this book is that I have noticed that there are basically two types of character:

1. **The realists:** the people I know, for example, from the fitness center. People who live in the present with every breath they take, who build houses, start businesses, and know exactly how to make things real and just do it.

2. **The dreamers:** On the other hand there is the dreamer, creating visions, wanting to change the world and acting on a more visionary level. But here I have discovered that it is precisely these people who have problems in making their dreams and ideas a reality. With this book, I want to help those people who have, so far, never dared to turn their dreams into just that.

That is easier than it sounds, but only if you also know the right moves. As in sports and at the gym, dreamers need a coach to offer some of his know-how and information on the methods we need to use to achieve our goals. There are a number of character traits in dreamers which I have come across again and again. For example, many of them use their dream to isolate themselves from their environment and often keep the dream to themselves.

They often think that if they only had enough money, the right contacts or other things, then they could make their dream work. They forget the most important thing! They forget that they will still need the right advice and do not think to look for a coach!

No success without a coach

When we think of the Australian Open or Wimbledon, whether it is Rafael Nadal or Serena Williams or Roger Federer, somewhere at courtside or in the stands sits the trainer, offering all kinds of guidance and support which can help to win the match and produce a player of world class. The job of a coach is to provide a little help, giving the player that edge which means crossing the fine line between success and failure. Trainers, even when they are not called such, can be found everywhere, in art, in business or in engineering. In all these disciplines, the trainer gives the instructions that enable his student to take the vital steps to cross this line.

For dream development and the realization of a dream, those **steps** are crucial!

If I tell someone that he should go to the first floor, but I do not show him where the stairs are, there is no way for him to get there. However, if I tell him where the stairs are, then it's very easy. It is the same with dreams. He who does not know the right steps cannot realize his dream.

There are many dreamers who dream to themselves. This book should be a training manual for all those who want to realize their dreams and have not yet taken steps towards doing so. Often, only small hints are necessary in order to realize how much energy there is in each of us and to use our gift of transforming thoughts into reality, just as the legendary King Midas once turned everything that he touched into gold.

It is very important to fully engage in this training and understand the instructions properly. Dreamers are loners and think they can do it all on their own. They do not think that even stars such as Roger Federer have coaches and also replace these trainers from time to time. Dreamers must look for a coach.

When talking about dream resources, many think of money, contacts or premises, but no one thinks to look for a coach!

In my professional and personal life, I have achieved much. All of it started with a dream. It is a fact that everyone can do it!

With this book, I want to be your coach, to guide you through the first steps to realizing your dreams and to give plenty of important advice for dreamers.

A wise man needs only a hint.

FLUMINA DE VENTRE EIUS FLUENT AQUAE VIVAE

Out of his belly shall flow rivers of living water.

John 7:38

Everything we dream, do and want to create—all comes from within ourselves. Each of us has the energy and the power to change our world at any time!

The Butterfly Effect on Dreams

Dreams hold mysterious but very powerful dynamics and forces. For decades the theory of the butterfly effect[i] has existed in science. This states that the flapping of a butterfly's wings in Japan is enough to trigger a hurricane on the other side of the world in South America.

This theory, which is supported by many scientists, not only shows that everything in our world is connected, but above all, that every little cause has a huge (and infinite!) effect.

Anyone who follows his dreams, even if he or she starts out with small steps or small changes in his or her life, will be surprised to see the positive results this may have for him or her in the future!

The butterfly effect is probably one of the most important truths by which our world works. This may begin to sound repetitive, but this principle really is found in every situation in our lives and therefore we will return to the butterfly effect several more times in this book. Once you understand that the butterfly effect exists **everywhere**, you can use this knowledge to achieve your goals.

The butterfly effect is not just present in weather phenomena. If you look closely, this principle exists in every situation and in every process in our world.

- A newborn child may have hundreds, thousands, hundreds of thousands and even billions of descendants.

- A single sneeze in an airplane can infect all the other passengers and make them sick.

- A single disease bacterium can be the trigger for a pandemic in an entire city or region (or the whole world: bird flu, foot and mouth disease...)

- The spread of AIDS works on the same principle. A single infected person, who has sexual contact with just a few people, may infect half a town. Of course, it would not be easy to trace this epidemic back to this person, because the connection between him and the other infected people is lost with distance and the passing of time.

- A small movement with your foot on the brake pedal slows down a car from 300 km/h to 0.

- Rudolf Diesel invented the diesel engine a mere 100 years ago, yet this now supplies whole sectors of industry, drives the development of diesel-powered transport and modern shipping of freight and supports globalization.

- A half a centimeter change on the wheel of a 500 meter long tanker moves the huge, skyscraper-high rudder at the rear, and thus the whole tanker changes course and may arrive in Rio instead of New York.

- If I write an article and I press the mouse button to publish this article on the internet, in theory, the majority of mankind has access to it. No one can tell who reads the article or what impact this will have on him, others or society as a whole.

- At the flick of a single light switch, hundreds or thousands of lamps can be turned on and off in a factory, the workers can work under good lighting, the products of the factory are of high quality and therefore sell well and the electric company makes money.

- With voice-activated systems, one only needs to speak, to turn the light or other devices on or off.

- A farmer named Hargassner[ii] in my neighborhood in Upper Austria developed a small modification for pellet stoves and started to sell them on his own farm. Today there is a factory assembly line, several hundred meters long, in which the furnaces are produced in series.

- The then-unemployed J.K. Rowling had originally intended to write a story for her children. However, her writing attracted far more attention than she expected and is now known around the world under the title of Harry Potter. A whole series of books, movies and merchandise followed, fan clubs were founded and countless authors were encouraged to write similar stories.

- The modern civil rights activist, Rosa Parks, refused in 1955 to give up her seat on the bus for a white man. With this seemingly insignificant decision, she sparked the Montgomery Bus Boycott organized by Martin Luther King and numerous protest movements and subsequent legal proceedings, which eventually led to the end of racial discrimination in the United States.

- In the first half of the 20th century, Mahatma Gandhi organized a variety of non-violent protest actions against the British colonial power, thus promoting the independence movement and finally bringing about the independence of India, the largest democracy in the world today.

A real sense of the power of the butterfly effect can often be obtained only if you seriously think about where the butterfly effect has already occurred in your own life story. Therefore, it is important to ask yourself the following question:

Where has the butterfly effect already occurred in my life story?

In other words, which seemingly trivial actions or deeds on my part had major consequences for me and changed my life or my environment as a result?

The butterfly usually does not see the hurricane coming...

Although many people are aware of the butterfly effect and that it can be found everywhere, it is often difficult for them to relate this principle to their own lives. They do not see where and when they have already done small things that have had a big impact. There's a very simple reason for that.

Our world is so vast and complex that we simply cannot understand the consequences of our actions in most cases. The actions and consequences are often **spatially** and **temporally** far apart.

Here lies the rub. The butterfly effect is everywhere, but because the consequences are not immediately visible or cannot be traced, we are not aware of them. That is why we easily lose faith in the power of our seemingly minor acts.

- Someone who has children perhaps will live to see his grandchildren and great grandchildren, but he will not be able see all his descendants in subsequent generations.

- Whoever develops an invention today, cannot imagine what people will be able to do 100 years hence. Some inventors are even ahead of their time. Other inventions may not yet have come to fruition, but may inspire future inventors to further developments, which in turn could conquer the world.

- An author who writes a book cannot see who this book inspires and what it might move the reader to do, as they are often based in other countries, or the inspiration may not be seized upon until many years later and by then can no longer be traced back to the book. We do not know today, for example, exactly what Nostradamus wanted to convey with his writings. But today, hundreds of years later, his texts appear again and again, causing people to weave conspiracy theories, to write articles or to bunker down in bomb shelters and hoard food supplies.

- Famous musicians are indeed aware that they have fan clubs in many countries, but they do not know how many fans there are exactly, and neither do they know about the regional events that are organized by their fans, as they are simply not their principal focus.

- Most people pay taxes and everyone makes a small contribution, but almost no one knows exactly how the money is used by the state (schools, public transport, social welfare, military).

- Whoever buys a product today, whatever it may be, performs only a brief transaction at the supermarket checkout. However, he cannot see how much is paid out in wages, how many companies stay in business, how many families are malnourished and the economic cycles which are kept in motion because of this fleeting transaction.

We rarely become aware of the consequences of our actions, but the fact is: **Everything** we do **has** an impact!

In quantum physics, there are even theories that state that simply observing a molecule with the human eye has eternal consequences!

All our actions have **eternal** consequences!

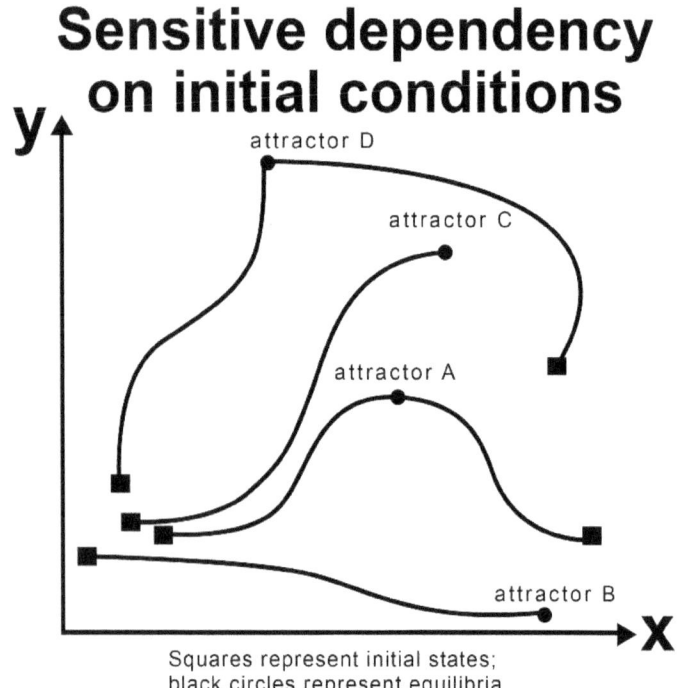

Squares represent initial states; black circles represent equilibria

All processes in this world and their results are extremely sensitive, depending on the initial conditions and influencing factors during the course of these processes. The actions we take and the process of taking actions are crucial, however small they may be.

"One of the surprising consequences of the modern version of the Darwinian theory is that apparently trivial tiny influences on survival probability can have a major impact on evolution. This is because of the enormous time available for such influences to make themselves felt."

>Richard Dawkins, Charles Simonyi Professor for the Public Understanding of Science at Oxford University

Homeless in India

I was living on the street, this in the middle of India, in one of the poorest regions of the world. Although my father's family was wealthy, after the Hindu inheritance law and my mother's decision to remain a Christian, after the death of my father we had nothing. And so from an early age I learned to fend for myself. Day after day I had to beg for a crust of bread to keep me going till the evening at least. I could not expect any help from anyone. I didn't know where the next meal was coming from or when it was coming. At the same time, I was a young man full of energy, who wanted to see the world. Should I have been having such ideas? In the 1970s, India was a country rich in culture—but certainly not rich in opportunities.

It was a long time before my mother was able to find a job and provide for our family. But even later, when my mother had a job again and I attended a hotel college, I worked in the evenings as a waiter to support my family. My hard work paid off and I was able to start in a luxury hotel in Bombay, where I was soon promoted to hotel manager. I was 23 and in Indian terms, I had made it. Actually, I could have stayed in that position, but what I did not know was that my sister had other plans for me.

She had always thought that I should see the world and go abroad. When she read an advertisement in the newspaper about an international scholarship in Europe sponsored by the United Nations, she signed me up without my knowledge. Before I knew exactly what it was actually about, I was going through an elaborate selection process. However, my chances seemed slim, because in India it was then the national sport to apply for scholarships abroad, and so I was not the only one who responded to the ad.

As I learned later, no fewer than 6000 young Indians had applied with me for the scholarship. 6000 young Indians who wanted what I wanted! Many of them had advantages, were from wealthier families, had a better education than I, and importantly had political contacts.

After a very long selection phase only 7 of the original 6000 were invited to undergo in-depth interviews. One of them was me, but even here, my chances seemed slim. The other six were all sons of politicians or Indian corporate magnates. All I had was my idealism to be able to put myself through a course of study in Austria and to take a step forward. As I sat in the waiting room where the final candidates were brought to one-on-one interviews, I said a prayer. I left it in God's hands as to whether I should go to Europe or not. That was my butterfly effect. To the great surprise of all, I got the scholarship!

"If you will it, it is no dream!"

Theodor Herzl

It always starts with a dream.

The second key step is **really** to want to realize this dream. If you really want something, then it is no longer a dream, but a reality.

Whoever sets goals should ask himself right from the start, why he wants to achieve these objectives and whether he is prepared to put his heart and soul into making it a reality. He who is really serious about realizing a dream and goes about it with real conviction, is already halfway there.

When you **will** it, it is no longer just a dream!

Thousands of years of human history and more happened just because people had dreams and were determined to fulfill them!

3 Ds

Dreams without deeds are dead

Deeds make our dreams dance

Thinking about dreams and imagining the wonderful visions are good first steps to directing your own consciousness in the right direction. But if we do not take action, then our dreams will die. On the other hand, deeds can make our dreams dance!

If you want to realize your dreams, act now!

Whoever walks down the street, sits on the bus listening to his neighbor, or asks about the dreams of other people in conversations with friends and family, will quickly realize that everyone dreams. But if statistics were compiled showing how many people actually live their dreams, even for one day, the proportion of people would be very low.

Most people have dreams but do nothing to realize them. Happiness is given to those who act and put something in place to reach their goals, because it does not happen by itself and there's a good reason for that. The reason is one of the central universal secrets that make up our world and has always shaped it.

To put it very simply, <u>we reap what we sow</u>. He who stands still and always stays within his own comfort zone, will remain there. Dreams want to dance and feel magically attracted by motion. A person who moves his life forward through action will be surprised how quickly opportunities and help will appear and sometimes be offered out of the blue, which can bring us significantly closer to our goal.

Again, the butterfly effect is shown very clearly. For example, a person takes a different route to work than usual, just once, and maybe discovers something that he has never seen before or maybe wins a new major client on the train which takes his business to a new level.

People who always go to the same events will always meet the same people. However, those people who attend events other than the ones they would normally attend, may meet some very interesting people or even his or her great love.

Many young entrepreneurs and inventors who only fish in their own pond and wait for the large investor might be surprised at the success to be had if they spoke to their business advisor about their ideas, instead of just talking to colleagues about their business ideas.

The Domino Effect

He who taps a stone, must expect many stones to start rolling.

Many people feel helpless and think they do not have the power to make their own dreams come true. They often overlook the fact that even the tiniest action triggers consequences and reactions. Even the smallest acts can trigger hundreds or even thousands of chain reactions and therefore influence or fundamentally change our own future or the future of others. How diverse and plentiful these consequences may be in retrospect, can be seen if you ask yourself questions such as, "What would have happened if..." if, for example, we look back at the history of mankind. For example, through observing nature, our ancestors in the Stone Age evidently discovered how to make fire or that wild plants can be domesticated in order to increase food security, which had consequences for the whole of humanity, something our primitive ancestors probably could not imagine even in their wildest fantasies. Would the story have been different if the steam engine had not begun its triumphal march in the 18th century, but even in ancient Egypt? In fact, there is some evidence to suggest that the Egyptian engineer and mathematician, Hero of Alexandria, discovered the operating principle of a steam engine, but just did not know how to use it. Could the Industrial Revolution really have begun 2000 years earlier?

Of course, when we look at the past, we cannot change anything and no one can say with any certainty what would have happened if things had been different. But this view of the past helps us understand what huge potential there is in small changes, inventions, and especially actions. Although we cannot change the past, the future is still unwritten and a man who topples just one domino in his life can expect to move mountains.

As elsewhere, the butterfly effect is evident once again, because even the smallest of actions can sometimes have major consequences.

In an atomic bomb, the initial trigger in comparison to the actual explosion is minimal. Even within the atomic bomb, a real chain reaction occurs that eventually leads to the nuclear explosion. Thus, this small initial trigger ensures devastating consequences. Often, only the direct damage of a nuclear explosion is seen as a consequence, but the area is contaminated for thousands of years, humans and animals fall ill, land is depopulated, politics change and the explosion has effects on the economy and culture of the country concerned, all because of a small initial spark that triggered a domino effect.

A similar chain reaction can also be observed in electricity generation, one of the peaceful uses of nuclear energy. During fission, an atom is split into several smaller particles. The released neutrons contribute to the splitting of other atoms, which in turn release neutrons. The process is repeated countless times, although only a single atom was split at the beginning. There are various types of nuclear power plants, but in all of these the process of the chain reaction is used to generate power, supplying millions of households with electricity.

In a steam locomotive, a similar chain reaction is deployed, which acts as the starting point for the butterfly effect. When carbon is added to the boiler, water is heated. This produces vapor, which in turn drives the piston and hence the engine under high pressure. The consequences of shoveling coal therefore is that goods and passengers can be transported from A to B, reaching people in time to do their jobs to feed their families, so that the station retailers can make profit, companies can export their products and much more, all because a small piece of coal was compressed and thrown into the boiler of a steam locomotive.

Snowball Effect

A chain reaction can turn into a snowball effect in some cases. In this case, the effect increases with each subsequent action or reaction. Thus, mighty hills can form from the tiniest speck of dust. You can very often see this effect in the field of communication. People who deal with social media are especially aware of the so-called viral effect. An interesting picture or a video that you have just sent to your friend can be viewed several times more on the Internet the next day, as it is distributed to a wider network of viewers, reaching a vast audience within a short time, and perhaps even conventional print media follows the trend and publishes the picture.

The Ripple Effect

Another effect, which is clearly related to the butterfly effect, is the ripple effect. Throwing a stone into water produces waves or ripples which spread out in all directions. It is impossible to throw a stone or any object into water without producing this effect. The ripples spread to the shore, go out again from the shore or overlap with other waves. But there is an infinite process, even if the waves may eventually no longer appear visible to the eye or seem to disappear within the other wave motions on the surface of the water.

A Nobody in Austria

Salzburg: I had actually arrived in Europe. What 5,999 others who had the same chance as I could not dream, I had dreamt and now also achieved. Simply because I was able to dream it, was I able to get the ball rolling and make it real.

The scholarship enabled me not only to go abroad and study, but in Salzburg I got to know and love Berta, the love of my life. She came from a small village in Upper Austria, where her parents had a farm. My early days in Austria were not easy. I was not allowed to take more than US $100 from India. I knew no one and had no idea how to earn my living. I did not understand German and I was living in another world entirely. However, I found ways to gain a foothold in this strange, new world.

I was fine, and yet something nagged at me: In the big scheme of things, I was nobody. It was the time of the Iron Curtain. The country was surrounded by the Eastern bloc and every day I read in the newspaper that more and more refugees wanted to come to the West. In addition, Austria was not a country of immigration. It was not America where you could make millions, even if you were just a bodybuilder like Arnold Schwarzenegger. The limits of what you could achieve were much higher in the U.S. and the hurdles on the way there seemed low. It was a completely different mentality. On the contrary, in Austria I always detected an aloofness towards strangers and thus also towards me. Nevertheless, I managed to get a job and eventually I became managing director of several restaurants and later of a luxury hotel.

Under no circumstances did I want Berta to one day think I was just an economic refugee and had only married her so that I could stay in Austria. My thoughts turned more and more to finding a new purpose in my life. Out of the blue, my sister gave me an idea, as if she could read my thoughts. At the time, she was Consul General in Israel. Again and again she told me about what was going on outside the embassy, until I started to listen. In front of her office, people camped out through the night to get a Green Card. She thought I was a fool for not seizing such an opportunity, indeed not even considering it. Eventually, I could no longer ignore her advice and I got myself a Green Card.

Ask, Pursue, Act
Questions show humility

He who wants to realize his dreams, must be willing to ask. No one is born with all the knowledge in the world. Even the biggest and brightest minds in the world today had coaches and teachers and knew where to find information. The transmission of knowledge is one of the most important keys to human development.

No one who drives a car today, who uses a lighter or a computer or surfs the Internet or even flies to the moon with a rocket, can do this because he was born intelligent or skilled enough to do so. We all now depend on inventions developed over the last 2000 years and indeed long before. Before people were able to build highways, someone had to invent the wheel thousands of years ago. Today, these and other inventions are accessible to the descendants of these inventors, inventions which every human being can use. Through schools, the Internet and our scientific heritage, it is possible for us to build on this knowledge, even if we take much for granted.

Anyone who wants to pursue his dreams must be willing to ask. The quest for answers and for knowledge reveals a hidden secret: He who asks, shows humility! And when you show humility to the world, doors will open.

Only an arrogant and selfish man does not ask, because he is afraid that he will betray his lack of knowledge in comparison to others. The question holds a hidden key in itself, for the moment we ask questions, we demonstrate humility before the miracle which is the world we live in. Ask, ask, ask! Who can provide the answers to help me live my dream? Ask and prove your humility to the world.

Very well-known is the story of Steve Jobs, one of the founders of today's technology corporation, Apple. When he was still in school, he was asked to carry out a project in his class. He had an idea, but no parts for it. However, he knew where he could get the parts. So he grabbed a phone book and called Bill Hewlett, the CEO of Hewlett Packard, and asked him if he could get a few spare parts from HP printers, which he wanted to use in his school project. The manager was impressed by the call from the young Steve Jobs. Not only did he send him the requested parts, but also offered him a summer job in his company, after which one can assume that many more doors opened for him.

Asking questions shows that you are serious in pursuing your dream, for the answers to these questions could hold the key to achieving your goals. Finally, it is important to use these answers and to turn them into action!

HHH or Redwood Principle

The redwood trees in California are among the largest trees on earth. They reach a height of up to 110 meters or more and have a girth of up to 17 meters. However, while looking at these majestic trees we only perceive what we can see on the surface. The redwood trees can actually only reach these breathtaking heights by forming a structure of strong roots under the earth. The roots often take up a huge area around the trees.

People who aim high and dream big must also pay attention to establishing roots. My son Clemens Öllinger-Guptara has coined the phrase "from head to heart to hands" to describe this. Dreams start in the mind and then must first reach the heart before the hands can be used to actually make dreams reality.

Unfortunately, many dreamers forget this essential intermediate step to first let their heart speak before they use their hands to develop an idea. Once an idea has taken shape in their head, they try to turn this idea into immediate results. Including the heart in your plans can instill passion and a lot more energy into pursuing your dream, thus giving you an additional boost, but also that necessary extra bit of endurance. Anyone who follows his dreams from the heart will find it easier to overcome the forthcoming challenges.

Therefore:

1. Head
2. Heart
and only then the hands!

Whatever you DO and WHY you do it makes a difference.

Heart = Faith

Of course, faith is directly related to the heart. The position of the heart is far more important than the movement of the heart when you have a dream!

The belief in a thing can be a far greater lever than many actions that are not carried through with great conviction.

When it comes to the realization of your dream, you must first position your heart precisely and ask yourself some questions.

What does my dream look like exactly?
What does the path to my dream look like?
Is realizing this dream close to my heart?

The positioning of the heart and the belief in a thing is so important, because the path is strewn with many obstacles and distractions. You will meet people who will tell you that this can never work or who want to show you a way in which it could supposedly work faster.

When taking any of these small decisions you must ask your heart which path to take or not to take, because in many cases these supposedly faster ways turn out to be diversions towards secondary goals that we did not originally want to achieve. Many dreamers lose sight of their intended goal here, wasting a lot of time and energy. There is a danger that our own dreams may be replaced by less important, secondary goals.

The principle of faith is found in all situations. If a driver does not believe that his car stops when he puts his foot on the brake pedal and therefore he does not hit the brakes, the car will not stop.

If a pilot does not believe that the plane will take off and therefore does not trust himself to accelerate the plane down the runway, the plane will never take off. Even worse, if it is already halfway in the air, but he does not believe that he can fly any further and he stops accelerating the plane...

Anyone who does not believe that small causes have large effects can never achieve his dreams.

This belief is the basic requirement for a dreamer to build a bridge to reality.

"Whatever you can do or dream you can, begin it!"

William Hutchinson Murray

Or as the author Paulo Coelho states in his worldwide success, *The Alchemist:*[iii] "When you really want something, the whole universe conspires in helping you to achieve it." Similarly, it did not occur to the Brazilian, Coelho, that all beginnings are accompanied by invisible, good luck dynamics. Beginner's luck is only for those who are brave and start to pursue their dream!

This beginner's luck and the reason why doors and paths suddenly open once a dreamer begins to work on his dream and begins something, can also be explained in a much more down-to-earth and easier way:

Anyone who moves in a <u>new</u> direction and does things he has never done before will automatically get to know new people, gain new insights and also find sponsors and partners who can and want to help them achieve the dream. This help does not come out of nowhere! It was always there! The dreamer has simply never taken advantage of it before.

Often our greatest helpers are sitting right next to us, but how can they help us if we do not tell them about our dream—indeed if they have no idea that we have a dream at all?

"As soon as the spirit is directed at a goal, much comes to meet it."

"Circumstances do not define us, we define our circumstances."

"To live in the Idea, means to treat the impossible as if it were possible."

"Knowing is not enough; we must apply. Willing is not enough; we must do."

Johann Wolfgang von Goethe

The Lever Principle

> "Give me a lever long enough and a fulcrum
> on which to place it and I shall move the world. "

Archimedes

Many of us have heard about the Greek scholar Archimedes in mathematics and physics. Even if we are not particularly interested in mathematics and physics, a famous phrase about Archimedes' lever principle may have stuck in our memory.

"Give me a lever long enough and a fulcrum on which to place it and I shall move the world."

Archimedes wanted to vividly highlight the enormous potential of the lever effect. Had Archimedes been able to stand in the universe in the right place and had he had the right lever, he could have moved the whole world.

Of course this principle cannot only be found in technology, it can also be applied to dreams. If you are facing a major challenge that is seemingly insurmountable, maybe you are just in the wrong place or do not have the right levers. Maybe you should change your location or select another lever to achieve your goal.

Newton's 3rd Law

Newton's third and perhaps most important law states:

"Every action creates a reaction."

Can we think of a reaction that is not preceded by any action!?

The average person thinks that if I do something then it's of no interest to anyone else, it has no effect, no consequences for my surroundings. This would be a mistake!

Every action causes a reaction! Not every reaction is immediate and not every reaction occurs at the same place, which is why we do not perceive many of the effects of our actions. But all our actions have an impact!

If I throw a ball against the wall, it bounces off it and falls to the ground due to gravity. If I change the rudder by only one degree on a ship on its way across the Atlantic, I might arrive in New York rather than Rio. If I have unprotected sex with a woman, the probability rises that a child is produced from it. When I fly by plane, CO_2 is released into the air and when I eat meat every day, there has to be someone somewhere in the world who makes more agricultural land available to produce feed for the cattle. If I rob a bank, I must expect to go to jail or at least to hide from the police for a very long time. When I change the elevator of an airplane, the plane does not land in Moscow but perhaps in Tokyo!

No action in this world is without a reaction!

2000 years have become reality

A remarkable example of what a huge impact small movements can have and how far-reaching and long-term dreams can be, is illustrated by the example of Israel and Theodor Herzl.

The area around present-day Israel has been inhabited for around 3000 years by Jews. After the kingdom was divided and conquered several times by different powers, it eventually came under Roman control. With the last revolt of the Jews against the Roman rulers in 135 AD, the Diaspora began (if not before), whereupon the Jewish population was dispersed across the globe over the centuries and the former Jewish regions in the Levant changed hands amongst various kingdoms. After around 2000 years of these movements, Israel no longer existed.

The Jews often found it difficult to settle, since their lives often involved persecution and chronic insecurity. Every prayer of the Jews, therefore, included the sentence: "Next year in our homeland."

Theodor Herzl, a Jewish journalist who lived in what was then Austria-Hungary, created the vision of a separate Jewish state in the 19th century, which he described in his 1896 book *The Jewish State*.[iv] A homeland for the Jewish people should be created in the regions where they had formerly settled.

But that was not enough. Theodor Herzl found kindred spirits, made contacts in politics and business, organized the first World Zionist Congress and even founded organizations whose intention was to buy land in Palestine and support the settlement of Jews. In his novel *Old New Land*ᵛ, he coined the slogan

"If you will it, it is no dream."

As early as 1903 the first Jewish families settled back in Palestine, although it was a far cry from an official state of Israel in the region. After the First World War and the end of Ottoman rule, the countries of the League of Nations campaigned for the creation of a Jewish state. The mandated power was Britain. It was followed by several waves of settlement in the region. After the Second World War and after the British Mandate for Palestine had expired in 1948, the modern state of Israel was proclaimed, which quickly led to war with the neighboring states. However, when a birth takes place, a birth takes place, even if it is associated with pain. Today, the modern State of Israel is considered one of the wealthiest in the world.

Theodor Herzl did not live to see this. He died in 1904, but his movement which he created and organized at that time, had unforeseen consequences that continue to reverberate far beyond his lifetime and will do so far into the future. He started something unique in the history of mankind. A country that has not existed for 2000 years was born again, with the same original language, the same religion and the same original people. A 2000-year-old dream has become a reality because people wanted it to.

In the sentence "If you want it, it's not a dream," Theodor Herzl stresses an important point for dreamers, because this is precisely the point that turns a dream into reality. **It is the will that counts!**

Theodor Herzl was not a theorist, a philosopher or a great orator, but he achieved his goal: He created an entire country from a dream.

Clueless in America

Although I was doing OK and I had no reason from a financial point of view to leave Austria, I decided to go to America. I wanted to make a career for myself, something I could not do in Austria. I had to leave the love of my life in Austria for the time being. I thought to myself, if she really loves me, she will follow me to America.

The so-called New World was indeed a whole new world for me. Exciting and thrilling, but also strange and yet challenging. Again, I knew no one here, had no friends and no idea how I should make money. At least I already knew the language. I wanted to pursue a professional career, all I needed was the profession. Based on my training and previous experience, I applied for jobs in the hospitality industry.

I started as a waiter, although I had already been Hotel Manager at the Intercontinental Hotel Bombay and had worked in restaurants and hotels in Salzburg as a manager. The reason was that I would have enough time to visit Berta in Austria in the meantime. As a waiter, it was possible for me to work just a few days during the week, but even these small beginnings set off a chain reaction. Later I was able to make contacts with tourism organizations, where I rose through the ranks.

*America was completely different from anything I had seen before. I knew that if I worked hard, I could make a career. For 20 years I remained in the hospitality and tourism sector. I had a feeling that I had achieved what many might describe as the American Dream, but it was **my** dream and I had lived it. In the end, I was very successful.*

Just one thing in my life clouded my joy—Berta was not there. She stayed in Europe all those years and we only saw each other occasionally. Meanwhile, I sensed that I couldn't convince her and I would have to return to her in Upper Austria sooner or later.

VAT

Most of us know or have at least seen on television how cars are made, so let's just imagine that we are in a Porsche car factory. Hundreds and thousands of people work intensely with computers and machines in factories like this one. According to the assembly line principle, a vehicle manufactured here passes through the various stations and often becomes a complete car ready to roll off the assembly line in just hours. But to actually find a buyer, it still needs to go through a final station, because at the end of the assembly line a worker is waiting who has the task of cleaning the vehicle and polishing the paint. This task does not necessarily contribute to the production of the actual vehicle, but this last step is as important as all the previous ones, since it is here that the vehicle is polished up and becomes ready for the customer.

At first glance, the last worker on the assembly line performs a minor task that is actually no longer part of the production process, because the car already appears to be finished. However, if the sports car is not polished, no one buys it. The worker polishes the car and adds even modest value. He did not re-invent the wheel, but only added a little value.

Similarly, no other step in the assembly line process can be left out. Each adds a little value to it. In turn, the butterfly effect also occurs here. The first worker may only tighten 2 screws on a plate at the very start of the line and may never see the finished work at the other end of the hall. And yet, his small task is vital to building a complete car at the end. A very small task thus has huge implications.

The added value principle can be applied to a wide variety of areas and projects and can of course also be used in the realization of dreams. Dreamers always think they must create something marvelously innovative and re-invent the wheel, but that's not true!

Some of the largest companies in the world were built on a business model in which only modest additional value was added to existing products.

Anyone who wants to achieve great things, should therefore not only make sure they create something new, but above all recognize how to improve things. Here again, we can see the butterfly effect.

Be it the internet, YouTube, Twitter, Tesla or Facebook or Google or 3D printing—the successful inventions of the world are mostly just improvements on existing things on which they are based.

No invention in human history was entirely new. There have always been things that have been based on existing inventions or knowledge or have merged several inventions to create a new product. In most cases, it is evident that it was only a small improvement, albeit with major consequences.

KISS

Keep **i**t **s**imple, **s**tupid!

One of the most important rules of being successful is to keep things simple! No matter what you plan, simplicity should retain its value.

Anyone can make something sound complex and create elaborate presentations, but are they relevant? Is it all about addressing a small, highly educated elite, which then only understands about 20% of what you want to say?

Or is it about selling—products, services, a message? Is it about reaching as many people as possible?

The fast food chain McDonald's[vi] was founded in California in 1940. In the following years and decades, the company enjoyed rapid expansion not only in the U.S. but also around the world. With approximately 35,000 restaurants worldwide and sales beyond the 27 billion dollar mark, McDonald's is among the largest restaurant chains in the world. But what could be behind this phenomenal expansion? One factor has certainly contributed significantly to its success. From the very beginning, the founders Richard and Maurice McDonald were anxious to keep it simple and straightforward. They were wise enough to take the KISS principle into account. If a guest comes to McDonald's, he doesn't need a qualification to decipher the menu. All that is required is to point to menu number 2 or 3 and you get what you want, to eat in or take out!

It's not rocket science!

Respect simplicity

There is a misconception of many inventors, developers and dreamers that ideas need to be made as complex and involved as possible to give the impression of quality and also to make it difficult to copy.

To design ideas so that they can be reproduced as quickly as possible is much more important. A system that can be adopted across the globe 1:1 has the potential to be transformed into a billion dollar business or reach billions of people within a very short time. We can see that when we look at successful brands such as IKEA, Facebook or McDonald's.

What seems simple and profound can change the world!

Decision & Commitment

Until someone actually sees the path ahead and commits to following it, he will tend to hesitate and the temptation to turn back is often too great.

However a fundamental truth lies behind all initiatives. If you ignore this, you will also destroy countless ideas and infinite plans.

At the moment someone definitely commits to his objective, fate shall take its course!

As soon as you will it, it is no longer a dream!

7-Step Mantra

A mantra is an incredibly good method for us to mentally to go along with a dream and to create, above all, a change in ourselves. Many people believe that mantras are something very spiritual and are therefore only to be performed by priests or spiritual guides. But here again, it is the simplicity that often has the biggest impact.

"Float like a butterfly, sting like a bee"

This sentence, which describes the fighting style of the boxer Muhammad Ali, is a mantra and is still used by boxers and even other people by being repeated over and over to mentally focus on a single objective.

1. **Decide:** It is important to recognize and to seriously commit to our goal

2. **Indoctrinate:** Repeating our motto over and over again promotes indoctrination. This ritual should be repeated every 3 or 4 hours, every day.

3. **Dance:** In the end, the spoken sentence creates a rhythm to which one moves and dances.

4. **Determine:** Success will only come to those who talk about and believe in their dreams and thus decide and determine that they will come true.

5. **Ask:** In this step it is important to ask all resources, friends, important contacts and nature for support.

6. **Do:** Now actions can be taken!

7. **Fulfillment:** The dream begins to come true.

"Whatever you can do or dream you can, begin it. Boldness has genius, power and magic in it!"

> Mountaineer William Hutchinson Murray (1913-1996), from his 1951 book *The Scottish Himalayan Expedition*

All sorts of things happen to help anyone who is committed to his cause; otherwise they would never happen in the first place. A whole stream of events follows on from the initial decision and opens unexpected doors. Contacts and material support arrive from sources you would never have dreamed of. (Serendipity)*

*The Serendipity Principle[vii] or "fate" is a term which describes the principle of "finding something without ever having looked for it." A serendipitous moment is often described as a lucky coincidence. Chase your dreams, and you will experience many such moments.

That's a promise!

The Tipping Point

Those who take an interest in the butterfly effect and observe it in many situations will find that there is always a critical turning point in trends, social phenomena, ideas and other things, whenever a small movement transforms into an unstoppable bushfire that spreads at a furious rate and triggers more and more chain reactions.

This critical turning point is described by Malcolm Gladwell as the "Tipping Point."[viii] This is the critical boiling point at which water becomes vapor, a virus turns into an epidemic and a product idea or a trend or a small association turns into an international movement is crucial for the achievement of dreams and goals of all kinds.

A downside to this critical point is that you do not know in advance when it is reached and how far one needs to go to achieve the desired effect. Many dreamers often put a lot of time and energy into their projects, precisely in order to reach this critical turning point, but they feel they have to first tread water. They give up on their plans, since success simply does not happen. They may have only needed one more day, have had to convince just one person of their idea or maybe a single new design was all that was required to reach the critical point where an initially small idea gathers unstoppable momentum.

The process of achieving the critical turning point can be compared to a mountain on which you want to roll a bowling ball. If you try to roll the ball up to the top of the mountain, then this is an exceedingly grueling process and you will only make slow progress. However, when the ball exceeds the tipping point it rolls down the hill, gathers speed and becomes unstoppable. Besides the fact that you had to push the ball slowly up the mountain, the crucial factor in the rapid acceleration of the ball was the one millimeter push required at the top of the mountain peak to trigger its rapid descent into the valley.

The Tipping Point, where movements and trends take on unexpected dynamics, is often compared with an epidemic. Thus, such a trend virus can spread "successfully," but for it to spread, it is essential that the right people are infected by it. So we may assume that a new urban shoe brand can probably become established much faster if the shoes of the brand are worn by young people in Manhattan or London than if they are only worn by people in rural areas or outlying provinces. The people who are the multipliers of the trend virus need not even be particularly numerous. Many now well-known brands can recount that in their corporate history, they only had need for a small group of people who were well-suited to act as multipliers, to help drive the brand forward that one extra millimeter in order to gather enough momentum to become unstoppable. Last but not least, one often speaks of the critical mass that must be reached by information or an idea, so that it takes root in the public consciousness.

The energy drink producer Red Bull has also followed this concept from its very beginnings. In the early years of Red Bull, when the brand was not yet firmly established in the market, the brand was targeted at extreme athletes and thereby was able to reach its tipping point. Besides the fan effect associated with extreme sports athletes, where fans follow their every step and of course notice when their idols grab a can of Red Bull, the brand was also very successful in building the desired image which surrounds Red Bull to this day and has made it so successful. Strictly speaking, however, it was initially probably only a few extreme sports athletes that you could count on one hand, but they were enough to get the ball rolling.

The human mind cannot comprehend exponential growth

A specific phenomenon is closely linked to the achievement of the critical point and the subsequent, rapidly spreading trend, which Federico Pistono[ix] describes in his book *Robots Will Steal Your Job But That's OK*. In his view, the human brain is not designed to actually understand and comprehend the consequences of exponential growth. People can basically understand linear growth, but exponential growth exceeds the human imagination.

A well-known example of the consequences of exponential growth, to which Pistono also refers, is the legend of Sissa ibn Dahir, who according to legend is said to have invented a chess game for the Indian ruler Shihram to entertain him. Overjoyed at having received the chess board, Sissa ibn Dahir granted the inventor a wish. The Brahmin was a modest man and only wished that the King fill the 64 squares of the chess board, one each day for 64 days, with rice grains which he would afterwards receive, but only so that the number of grains of rice on the second square were double that on the first, and so on. Thus, only a single grain of rice was placed on the first square, two grains of rice on the second square, four grains of rice on the third square, eight on the fourth and so on. The king laughed and granted his wish which had been received in good faith. After a few days however, it turned out that the granaries of the empire would probably be empty quite soon. For those who can do the actual calculation, you will find that there would be several trillion grains of rice on the last square of the chess game. King Shihram did not understand the concept of exponential growth either.

Exponential growth is also illustrated by examples of the Columbian exchange. Before the discovery of America by Columbus, numerous animals and plants, which are now considered commonplace, couldn't be found in the New World. However, the original populations of many of today's widely used animals and plants in the Americas were often very small.

We know for example that Columbus took only 8 pigs on his second voyage to the Caribbean in 1493. Twenty years later, 30,000 offspring were counted alone in Cuba and today millions of Americans would probably have to give up their beloved barbecue if those 8 pigs had not reached the New World hundreds of years ago.

Equally impressive is that the U.S. exports about 5 million tons of apples annually. Before Columbus, this fruit was unknown in America. It all started with just a few small seedlings from Europe.

If you reach the critical tipping point, prepare for exponential growth and not for linear growth!

The Multiplier Effect

Someone who recognizes the multiplier effect is never alone. The multiplier effect forms the basis of exponential growth—no matter whether it is a product, a brand or an idea or a societal concept. Understanding how this effect works provides an unstoppable way of spreading any innovation like wildfire around the world.

The multiplier effect can be seen particularly clearly in viral marketing. Whether it is through word of mouth or through social media channels, a good idea spreads rapidly, and above all—exponentially. For example, a YouTube video that you forward to a friend and which he also likes will be sent to maybe two other friends. The link to the video is in turn sent from those two friends to three other friends and shared with them. Although the link has therefore undergone only 3 forwarding phases, 10 people have already been reached and have taken note of the video. With each subsequent forwarding, the number of viewers may increase further.

Despite the internet, new media, and mobile communication devices, word of mouth is still seen as the best means to spread a message quickly and sustainably, for nothing sticks in the mind quite so much as a story told in person. In order for this to work, the story has only to be interesting. Whether it is an idea, a real life experience or a recommendation for the café on the corner where the latte macchiato tastes so good, there must always be an initiator of the message who tells it first hand, for the first time, to someone else. If it is interesting enough it will be passed on, told to other friends and sometimes even told to colleagues or at a family celebration. More people hear about it, want to know more about it, ask for the café and finally go along to the café, to see for themselves how the macchiato really tastes.

Liz Wiseman, Lois Allen and Elise Foster, who describe the multiplier effect in detail in their book[x], also point out that this effect can be found in many areas of life, for example, in modern learning environments. Previously, the teacher was merely seen as the person in the school who could impart knowledge to the pupils. Today, other concepts are being applied, because it has been recognized that knowledge spreads easily and quickly. To take an example, the first 5 students receive the information and in turn every student conveys this to 5 groups, each with 5 other students. This way, 30 students could be reached in a very short time. These 30 students could theoretically pass on their acquired knowledge to another 5 students each, so that in a short time another 150 students have been reached. If they impart their knowledge in the same way, 750 students can benefit from the knowledge, which was initially only passed on from one teacher to 5 students. To achieve the same effect in the old way, the teacher would, however, require much more time.

Through the multiplier effect, then, a far greater number of people can be reached in less time. Anyone wishing to use the multiplier effect has to find the right people as the first multipliers to ensure that the first multiplications are set in motion.

In their book *The Multiplier Effect*, the three authors analyze two different types of people who can act as a role model. On the one hand, there are those who always want to be perceived as the most successful and smartest person in the room. Nevertheless, their overbearing presence destroys the basis for good ideas in the group, consumes energy, and allows no room for other talents and abilities to flourish. On the other hand, there are people who walk into a room with people and create sparks anywhere in the group. They use their knowledge effectively to convey it to others, in order to inspire talent and encourage others to believe in themselves. These people are true multipliers!

They know that they can achieve much more if they share knowledge in this way and encourage people to pursue their talents, interests and goals. It's amazing how much potential can be tapped and developed in people when they get the right motivation. Anyone who understands this type of motivation also recognizes that much quicker and more far-reaching results can be achieved than when everyone simply sticks to motivating themselves.

When good becomes the enemy of the better...

Anyone who wants to achieve goals often sees walls and obstacles ahead that need to be overcome. However, there are also many positive temptations in the early stages which may easily distract you from your journey. Anyone who follows a dream should know the following:

The **good** is the worst enemy of the **better**!

On the path to our goals there are always partial successes. Sometimes we even leave the path and achieve other goals that we did not initially plan to do. Before you know it, a sense of satisfaction sets in.

OK, I didn't make it to the world championship, but I still took part in the state championship. I may not have my dream house, but I still have a nice apartment and instead of the 20 pounds I wanted to lose, I still lost 10 pounds in weight.

That's good enough, isn't it?

Well, yes, but didn't we actually want to do better? Didn't we want to achieve more? These "good" successes usually don't have much to do with the goals we initially set. The good is the enemy of better.

Instead of continuing to work on our goals, we get distracted and move towards a situation with which we are satisfied.

Attention! Distraction!

Those who go into business to pursue their dreams there will quickly realize that many doors will open for them in a relatively short space of time. You receive invitations to various events and meetings, new contacts can be made and perhaps a lucrative sounding business model will be presented to you, which you are usually told to apply now rather than later in order to take advantage of developments in the market.

Just the prospect of quick money is often an incentive for taking a supposed shortcut, but a shortcut to where? What is the shortest path good for when it does not lead to where we wanted to go?

"You rarely have time for everything you want in this life, so you need to make choices. And hopefully your choices can come from a deep sense of who you are."

Fred Rogers

The Outlier Effect

With his descriptions of the outlier effect[xi], the author Malcolm Gladwell again claims that even the smallest differences in an environment can involve huge consequences. He compares, for example, the learning achievements of pupils in different urban schools in the U.S. and comes to the conclusion that students are more successful in some schools and learn more than others. However, that is not due to the pupils themselves being born intelligent or not but rather to the social environment in which they learn at their respective schools. Gladwell assumes that the different school environments cause the pupils to spend more or less time in school and thereby acquire more or less knowledge.

Likewise, this social phenomenon can also be seen if we look at the circumstances of elite athletes, prominent entrepreneurs or even musicians. Looking at the environment in which they grew up, it quickly becomes clear that their family already included athletes, entrepreneurs and musicians who influenced and probably encouraged them. Their interests and talents are literally already in their genes. This does not mean that others are not capable of such excellence, but those who enjoy the benefit of such an environment have the perfect opportunity to prosper.

Each one of us is strongly influenced by the environment in which he lives and grows up. Above all, our parents offer guidance along the way, but we also absorb information and attitudes from friends or other relatives and mentors whom we may encounter for brief periods in our life, but offer the right words to put us on the right path and boost our self-confidence to pursue our own dream. It may be then that the words of a relative, for example an uncle or a cousin who are of the opinion that the right conditions are in place to achieve our dream, are all we need to keep inspiring and encouraging us to never to lose sight of our goal.

Whether we like it or not, everyone takes onboard certain influences, inclinations and talents from their environment over a period of years. Even people who do not give the impression that they grew up in a very conducive environment, have had seminal experiences in their life or have spoken to people who have offered the right words at exactly the right time or have inspired them in another way, consciously or subconsciously, and have triggered a significant change in their life. It does not have to be relatives or friends. Maybe it was a stranger with whom we talked or who explained something to us or inspired us to expand our horizons, with major consequences in later life.

Our environment can hold the key to the dreams we dream and the resources we have available to turn them into reality. Therefore, it is both very important to look at our environment as well as to seek the contacts that prove positive for us. In many cases, simply changing our environment to seek new influences and inspiration has proven to be successful.

Metamorphosis

To fulfill a dream, it is often necessary to change yourself in order to overcome hurdles, to take on challenges and do things that others do not. Anyone who wants to fulfill a dream must be prepared to undergo a metamorphosis and a change, as a caterpillar does when it turns into a butterfly.

There are many pieces needed to complete this puzzle. If just one of the necessary building blocks is missing, the dream will never come true!

Metamorphosis take place everywhere in the world, every day, in nature, in business, in cities, in a cocoon, in water or in medicine.

- A brown cow needs green grass to turn it into tender red meat. If it does not, the metamorphosis cannot be completed and the result is different.

- If you want to bake a cake, you need to have all the ingredients, but you must mix them to form batter and place it in the oven. Without this change to the original form of the ingredients and the baking process, the ingredients will never turn into a cake.

- If you want to run a marathon, you must change your lifestyle well before and train to adjust mentally and physically to it.

- If you want to make a film, you need to first learn how to use a video camera.
- If you are still a student and you would like to get a job after school, you need to change your behavior in order to become an employee, since in a company there are other rules of behavior and skills required than those needed at school.
- If you want to give a successful presentation, you must learn what is important in self-presentation and practice speaking in front of other people.

It always comes down to doing different things in order to achieve different results. If you just keep doing the same things, you will only achieve the same results.

Anyone who wants to make a difference has to act differently.

Metamorphosis contra Agere

Change by opposite action

If you want change, you not only have to act differently, but also often to act in a contrary or opposite way. People who act differently to how they did before, will get different results.

If you do what is normal to you, and have had no success, you will continue to be unsuccessful if you do things the same way. Only he who acts differently and contrary to his normal thinking can take a different route and be successful.

He who wants to live his dreams needs to acquire a singularly positive mindset. In our "modern" society, we are often brought up in a rather negative way of thinking. Most things are done under pressure, tension, and through anxiety. In order to pursue a dream, it is necessary to open up and to find some positive motivation. Anxiety must become self-consciousness. An outward impression of self-confidence in your own ideals and objectives alone can often open many doors. Rather than subjecting yourself to pain, it's easier and better to do things that provide pleasure, is it not?

So! The first step to change and to metamorphosis is to think about exactly what the motivations are for the actions, steps and deeds in your life. If these are negatively influenced, they should be turned into positives. This is easier than you think! Even a donkey pulls a cart better when he gets a carrot held in front of his nose, rather than if he is beaten with a stick.

"Within me lies the power to change any moment...
... at any time!"

Raja Öllinger-Guptara

The moment that changes everything

On every farm there is normally a hay barn or hayloft where straw is stored. Usually those spaces do not have to meet stringent architectural requirements and as a result there are many leaks and gaps in the floorboards and walls through which sunlight can shine into the room. This happens over a period of years, even decades. Sunlight penetrates through the gaps in the wood, falls onto the straw and bathes the hayloft in an almost heavenly light, over years and indeed decades.

However, this seemingly permanent situation can change rapidly. If I catch such a ray of light with a magnifying glass, the light is concentrated and now falls more directly onto the straw. What happens? The straw heats up, quickly catches fire, and the whole hayloft or maybe the entire farmhouse together with the neighborhood burns down to its foundations.

This effect, which has a very destructive result in this example, can of course be channeled in other directions.

Everyone has the power to change any moment. At any time!

The more aware we are that we have the power to change any moment, and thus to influence the future today, the better we are able to make use of this opportunity.

The New York construction worker Wesley Autrey[xii] also seemed aware of this power when he was waiting for the subway at 137th and the corner of Broadway in January 2007 with his two daughters and noticed a man who had collapsed in the station, stumbled and fallen onto the tracks. Autrey did not hesitate and jumped onto the tracks after him. The lights of the oncoming subway train could already be seen as Autrey pulled the man into a small hollow under the platform, little more than 30 cm wide, and saved his life.

Of those present, only Wesley Autrey had realized that he was able to change this moment, because he wanted to and so he did!

"I have the power to change any moment. At any time!"

The consequences of this sentence are enormous!

Anyone who has seriously believed that he can change this moment has already done it.

No one is condemned to being unable to change anything. Everyone has the power to change any moment! And by changing the moment, we are not only changing the present but also the future. If only one person in the world becomes aware of this and realizes that he or she can change any moment, we have already achieved a lot, because from this a butterfly effect will be created! Everything depends on this single sentence.

"Everything can be taken from a man but one thing: the last of the human freedoms—to choose one's attitude in any given set of circumstances, to choose one's own way."

Victor Frankl

The Viennese psychiatrist and neurologist Victor Frankl was imprisoned in concentration camps for several years during the Second World War. During his detention, he observed inmates, and was also amongst those who helped other inmates, who comforted them, or gave them food, in spite of their own difficult situation. He was later to publish the above quotation. Frankl had seen that a person's freedom of choice cannot be taken even in captivity, where you would think it most likely to happen. Just consider then the opportunities for those who live in freedom!

When the active displaces the passive

The effect that every person can change any moment and thus change his future or the future of others can also be seen in simple situations in everyday life.

Many coffee houses and bars all over the world sometimes do very well from a special type of patron who has already long given up on improving his or her prospects. The long-term unemployed certainly have a raw deal, but only if they do not see their situation as a new beginning, but remain trapped in old patterns of behavior.

These patterns are often very monotonous. Many wonder, what is left for them to do? They spend valuable hours and days trying to sit in coffee houses and bars, drinking one beer after the other to pass the time. Others have reached a different point and entertain thoughts of suicide because they no longer find meaning in life, or they consider robbing a bank or other people. It happens thousands of times every day all over the world!

They would only have to recognize one truth in the world:
"I can change any moment – at any time!"

What we do with our lives is not up to others, industry, the economy or the welfare state—it is entirely up to us! Everyone has it in his own power to change the moment and do something different from what he has always done. This sentence cannot be repeated often enough, because it is so important! Change is the second step.

A construction worker who has lost his job due to a crisis in the construction industry and who has not been able find a job in a long time, can either complain for months about it and spend his time in the coffee house by flipping through newspapers or he can say to himself, "I want to change that now," and seek a change.

Most people are trapped in their rut because it also has something to do with their identity. "I've always been a construction worker, I am a construction worker and I will always remain a construction worker." Beliefs like these are often firmly entrenched.
Is there an alternative?

Yes, there is if you allow it! Nobody ever considers changing and performing a metamorphosis. Didn't I actually always want to be a painter or a poet or to help children? Are there not thousands of things that are burning deep inside of me and which I want to do? A career setback is the perfect opportunity for such a new beginning!

It's about moving from passivity to activity. If you only realize this, you will be surprised how quickly things can change. People who remain passive will stay trapped in their own thoughts, and these thoughts have unbelievable power—the realization that you yourself have the power to make decisions at any time, the power to follow the path of light or shadow, day or night, life or death!

Someone who is unemployed can either sit in the café and decide to keep drinking, or he can immediately ask the waiter if they want any help in the kitchen. Maybe he will get a rejection the first time around, but at least it is a positive action, and no action is without a reaction. For metamorphosis to occur, it is important to be ready for change.

A change in mindset

If you think of yourself as a manual worker and have not been happy doing this, try to change and say, "I'll try being a worker in the agricultural sector, because I have always been good at working with animals and plants." Or maybe a temporary worker in the restaurant business, as an artist, wandering minstrel, hairdresser... the possibilities are endless.

These are just a few simple examples of how everyone has it in his own hands to change every moment in his life immediately. The worst thing is to remain stuck in familiar thought patterns that have already proven to be unsuccessful in the past. Why should these thought patterns be helpful now? Why would they succeed?

The pension shock

Hundreds of thousands and probably millions of pensioners around the world are deeply frustrated due to their habitual thought patterns, simply because they cannot escape from these very familiar thought patterns or do not sincerely want to do so. You think to yourself, "I was always an official or an employee, and now I'm retired and am incapable of doing anything but sitting in front of the TV and waiting for lunch."

At that moment they are not aware of how many options they actually have. Retirement is not the end of active life. Strictly speaking, retirement is a purely human invention resulting from the economic and social development in the industrialized countries over the last 100 years. No law in the world dictates how retirees have to behave and certainly not that they should be passive, but the majority of people on pensions believe exactly that.

Anyone who thinks he can change this moment right now and with it his life, may have recognized the most important aspect in his life and may be open to other approaches, allowing a more active life, even if it's small things. I can help children cross the street safely. I can help in the kindergarten and read stories. I want to help people as a gardener, because most people in the city have no idea of gardening, but gardening has been my hobby for the past twenty years. I can go to schools and talk about my Australia trips in geography lessons, etc., and do something that makes me feel good.

Muscle training

Another situation in which it is plain to see how easy it is to use the power of decision making and change the moment immediately, is at the fitness center. Many people there rapidly employ a thought technique called flow thinking. They do their 30-minute workout with the usual four circuits, one after the other. Since these thought patterns come automatically to them, few people stop to realize that you can only train the same four muscles in this way. The body is not only made up of four muscles. You have to train the other muscles too.

Again, the metamorphosis can be applied very easily. Say to yourself, "Today is Tuesday, so I'm not doing these four training circuits, but I will deliberately try out the other training equipment, which I very rarely use, to strengthen the other muscles." It is the easiest thing in the world to do, but if you actually do it, you can use it to create changes in any situation.

If you only start to do little things differently in your job, you may have a lot more success, or be able to work more efficiently. Get out of this automatic way of thinking!

More exercises to raise awareness of the power of decision making

- At each intersection I have the option to go left, right, straight or even backwards.
- At the supermarket I can buy organic or chemically treated foods, packed in a paper bag or plastic.
- I can begrudgingly go to work or put a smile on my face in the morning.
- I can spend my lunch break at my desk as always or go out for once.
- When searching for a job, I can write applications at random or focus all my energy on a job that I really want.
- In everyday life, I can wear my everyday shoes or even my dress shoes.
- I can look down at the ground or I can give a friendly smile to passers-by, the shop assistant in the supermarket and the bus driver.
- If there are events in my city or anywhere else, I can say to myself that I would feel out of place there or I can just attend.

- I can watch TV or go out or draw a picture or write a song, read a book, etc.—the possibilities are endless.
- I can take the same daily newspaper or read the same newspaper on the internet as always or I can gain a completely different perspective from a magazine or a blog which I have never read before.
- I can drink coffee in the morning as always, even though it gives me heartburn, or I can drink a cup of tea instead.
- I can warm up TV dinners as always or I can try to cook for myself.
- I can rather keep out of the way of my boss or thank him for the good advice he has given me lately.
- I can be upset about the opinion of a friend on a particular issue or I can just try to understand why he is of this opinion and accept it.
- Instead of driving to work, I can cycle or take the bus.
- Although the weekend is almost over, I can still take a day trip or go to the museum.
- I can ignore a tourist who is obviously lost or I can approach him and ask if I can help.

At every moment, what I do and how I want to live the moment is always my decision! There are countless other such small examples you can use in everyday life. See how it feels even to do one thing differently and to make new choices that will have an impact on your life. It is best to look at things and situations that you are not really happy with and to see where you can try and do something different to the tired old norm. You will be surprised what effect this may have in the short term as well as the long term.

"Insanity: doing the same thing over and over again and expecting different results."

Albert Einstein

30 seconds that decide everything!

Lecturers, trainers and business people know that the first impression is crucial and can determine success or failure. Even in the first few minutes, though some experts believe that it is only 30 seconds in which we form a picture of the person in front of us and try, albeit subconsciously, to assess and classify it. This initial classification often sticks in our mind—regardless of whether it is accurate or not.

Whether it is a job interview, welcoming a new customer, consulting a new doctor for the first time or just casually coming into contact with a stranger, the first impression always counts!

We do not judge a person within seconds because of rudeness or a lack of genuine interest in others, but for quite practical reasons. The author Malcolm Gladwell describes in his book *Blink*[xiii] that we think without actually thinking, because we often do not have enough time to stop and think. If we are forced to judge a situation within seconds, our experiences, our set of beliefs and our values play a major role.

Too often, important decisions depend on the subconscious assessment that is made automatically within a few moments. However, if you are aware that all people judge and commit such situations to memory, you can also make use of this knowledge.

Control the moment!

Behind this power of subconsciously judging people or situations lies the risk of making the wrong decision on this basis. If we had all the relevant information about a situation, our decision would probably turn out to be completely different.

Making wrong decisions may hinder us on the way to achieving our goals. A good way to avoid the feelings and experiences based on judgment and therefore making wrong decisions is always to be aware of it. Especially in situations in which we need to act quickly or have only a short time to decide, we should remind ourselves that many of our assessments are made subconsciously and we might not have all the necessary information. To control the moment, we should, if possible, also seek as much information as is necessary. If the decision is still difficult, a gut feeling may yet be all that is needed to tip the scales.

"The domination of the moment is the domination of life."

>Marie Freifrau von Ebner-Eschenbach (1830–1916), Austrian storyteller and novelist

Act as if

If a change in thinking has taken place in your mind and you are aware of your dream, the next, even more important step arrives.

Act as if!

It is not enough to think differently, it is important also to act differently—yes, to be different!

Who prevents a dreamer from acting as if all his goals have already been achieved? What prevents someone who wants to be a pilot from buying or lending a pilot's uniform for a day strolling into an airport and having his picture taken with it in front of a plane or even in the cockpit? Such a photo should then be stuck onto the bathroom mirror or mounted somewhere where it will always be remembered!

Acting as if our dreams have come true helps us not only to change our own thinking, but to immerse ourselves into our dream situation. Before anyone can be a pilot, he firstly needs to believe that he is a pilot. As soon as I can see myself as a pilot, I will believe that I am a pilot.

The philosophy of "as if" was developed and formulated in the 19th and 20th centuries by the German philosopher Hans Vaihingen, based on the theories of Kant. It is a philosophy and personality technique that probably many of the world's best actors will know. A good Hollywood actor immerses himself in his role long before shooting begins, 24 hours per day. He tries to **be** the person and not just pretend, along with all the characteristics the role entails. The actor also remains in his role and as that person throughout filming. This technique is also known as method acting.

Pretending "as if" is one of the most important factors in realizing dreams!
It's best to start immediately!

A Nobody again in Austria

So that's the story so far. After a number of successful years in America, the focus of my life would shift to Europe once more. I had recognized that Berta could not imagine a life in the U.S. I had built the career I had dreamed of, but when I returned to Austria, I could not pursue it further. The area where Berta grew up was heavily dependent on agriculture. I was about 50 years old. Who would give me a job here? Even those people who wanted to give me a job could not, because I had no experience in agriculture. Once again, the chance to reinvent myself lay in front of me. Berta had taken over a farm from her parents, so I saw the opportunity to become the first Indian-born farmer in Austria. I had to teach myself everything and doubtless made a lot of mistakes. Driving a tractor, bringing in the harvest and managing the fields was certainly not easy, but only he who starts something can learn and reap the rewards, I thought to myself.

Gradually, I learned what was necessary in order to be successful as a farmer—how to manage fields, how to drive a tractor and how to bring in the harvest. Eventually I realized that agriculture alone was not enough for me. Our family lived in a small part of the big farmhouse in the middle of our land. In addition, there were many former stables and workers' quarters that stood empty. Valuable potential, I thought to myself. Before boredom had a chance to set in, I decided to utilize my experience from the hospitality sector again and set up holiday apartments in the farmhouse. Before starting this project I also had a dreamlike vision of today's Geinberg Suites, a lively place where people from all over the world could stay and live and where events should be held. Here, I also wanted to incorporate the Indian influences of my former home. Without this vision, it would have been impossible to relearn everything needed to renovate and refurbish the premises. But without the will to actually start, it would have been impossible to realize the vision. Again, I made many mistakes, but also learned from them. Today, the Geinberg Suites, which to a large extent I have created with my own hands, can be seen as an oriental oasis in the middle of the traditional Upper Austrian alpine landscape.

Although I may have found it difficult when I returned to Austria, an uncertain future lay ahead of me and I did not know what to do next, so I tried to see everything from a different perspective and to use my remaining opportunities!

HHH instead of "burning your tires"

From the head to the heart and hands. This principle deserves special attention and should always be applied. There are actually people who can create results in no time, but that is not necessarily a guarantee of success, since they only think about the figures and have the concept thought out in their head and realize it with their hands. Yet they have skipped the most important step in between—namely the heart.

Anyone who forgets his own heart and begins a project, although the project may mean little to him, can work as hard as he wants, complete all the milestones and complete as many checklists as he would like, yet the desired goal cannot be achieved in the way he would like and reaching the goal comes at the expense of his health or relationships. The Americans also call it "burning your tires." One can see that even the word "burnout" is not far off the mark here.

A dream must be desired and realized from the heart. Although the idea is born in the mind and is realized with the hands, the heart is always the sustaining force that helps to clear the way and provide courage and commitment.

How do we know whether the heart is with us?

You can feel it. More specifically, it is often more of a gut feeling to which you should listen. If you listen closely to it, then you know whether an action actually puts you on the right road to achieve your own goals or is just a detour or even a dead end.

Beware of opportunities!

On the way to our goals, perceived chances and opportunities are offered to us again and again which may be of some modest help in achieving our dreams and therefore sound tempting. As already mentioned, many doors and gates open when we are focused on our dreams. We meet people who want to help us and maybe receive invitations, without knowing exactly what the outcome might be.

If you want to change yourself, you have to do different things. Nevertheless, it is always important to keep an eye on our milestones and where we should focus, because the path to our goals is littered with many distractions and supposed opportunities. These demand our energy! They can also lead us astray.

For example, young entrepreneurs almost always look ahead to the many new contacts and invitations to fashionable events that their business brings with it, but almost always overlook the fact that they have neglected their core business or even their goal and their dream, because they put too much energy into their own perception of events.

The challenge is that we live in a world where many people live under pressure, but are also driven by greed or fear of missed opportunities. Everyone wants quick access to everything (and immediately). A guy gets into his car, rushes round to keep his appointments and goes from bank to bank to get a loan for his project. Then he finds out that he will not get the money, because the bank was not convinced by his plan. This is the first shock, i.e., he will not get a loan. His head drops and he gets frustrated (the belief is no longer there).

Had he taken his time and gained the knowledge and the belief that his steps would work, that his actions are bound to have an effect, then things would have been different. It is simply the law of physics.

What actions are the right ones for me?

To answer this question, the most important step is to stand back and to put your heart in the right place! Most dreamers do not position it correctly in order to be able to decide unequivocally later on where the heart says yes, and where it says no.

You have to allow yourself time to establish a foundation, to position yourself correctly and have the right belief, belief in the cause, belief in the dream, belief in the leverage effect, belief in the butterfly effect. Only when the heart is in the right place and the dreamer has faith can he overcome the inevitable rejections and hurdles.

Do I want to dream the dreams of others?

Many actions and distractions sound good. Sometimes someone shows us an easier, faster way. Maybe he is offering us the genuine prospect of being able to earn good money quickly or even to become famous. But it is very important at this point to keep the faith and follow your own dream and to listen to your own heart.

Everyone has their own dream. We quickly find ourselves in situations where we actually pursue or live the dream of another person, not our own. This dream is not meant for us, and therefore it will not make us happy, no matter how successful we are in pursuing it.

It is wonderful when friends, colleagues or acquaintances tell us about their dreams. However, their dream is special to them, not necessarily to us, because again, everyone has their own dream!

The lure of imitation

A different kind of lure often emerges here, namely, simply to copy a method that has already been working successfully for someone else. It is quite possible that you will succeed quite quickly by doing so, but if it is not your own dream, you will continue to feel unfulfilled. Imitating someone will always mean you are "playing catch up," because you are trying to copy others.

The secret of repetition

One of the most powerful secrets behind successful people who live out their dreams lies in repetition.

If we look at the achievements and works of athletes, musicians, poets, or entrepreneurs and visionaries, or if we see these people in the media or read about how they are awarded prizes or win medals, we are only witnessing a small part of their present existence. What we do not see are the many years that have preceded this achievement. After all, these people may not have had a complete set of skills and abilities right from the start.

They, too, repeat, repeat and repeat in order to be counted among the world's best!

Many athletes train for several hours a day, every day! Arnold Schwarzenegger has said that in his active days as a bodybuilder he would train 4-5 hours every day, continuously for six days a week. If he had missed training for even one day, he would have run the risk of losing the # 1 spot in the world.

If dreamers have a good idea, then many of them believe that it must work immediately, the very first time. However, success most often comes only on the umpteenth attempt. The example of Thomas Edison and his invention of the incandescent light bulb is world famous. He tried thousands of test materials before he found the right material for the filament, to enable the bulb to burn for long periods and thus make it marketable. He took those thousands of failures in stride, in order finally to reap the rewards. Persevering with thousands of experiments led him to success. At the same time, he found thousands of ways that did not work. Hardly anyone knows that during these innumerable tests he had incidentally discovered that electricity can also be distributed among several lamps.

The secret of repetition can also be found on other levels. Mixing mortar on construction sites, for example, requires experience. It requires the perfect mixture of water and cement. If too much or too little water is included, the mortar becomes either too hard or too soft. Experienced bricklayers on construction sites no longer need a measuring cup for making mortar, because through years of repeating the right proportion of cement and water it is already in their blood, so to speak.

Why is repetition so important?

As the old saying goes, practice makes perfect. But why? What is the secret? Why can't things always work perfectly the first time?

The answer to these questions lies in the fact that innovation can arise through repetition. Repetition creates the so-called innovative edge, the innovative know-how advantage which those who have not repeated something hundreds and thousands of times cannot have. For it is only with the repetition of a process, whether in technology, sports or personal development, that the weaknesses in the system can be recognized. You can still repair and improve and adapt subtle aspects in order to achieve the best result.

Even established processes, seemingly entrenched for decades, can be improved and evolved through repetition. In the 1960s, the high jump was already long established in international athletics and the record heights seemed to be approaching their limit. That was until a young athlete named Richard Fosbury found out, through repetition and training, that much higher jumps were possible by jumping backwards rather than feet first. Using this novel "Fosbury flop,"[xiv] he won gold at the 1968 Olympic Games in Mexico und invented a jumping technique which is now the standard. Without testing, training and repetition of this revolutionary innovation, this feat would not have been possible.

Innovations and enhancements that result by repeating something can also be found in small things. On our farm with its accompanying apartments, for example, I always had an old furnace that was fired with wood. For a long time, however, I was not convinced of the efficiency of the furnace. Again and again, I had to burn large amounts of wood and coal without supplying the desired heat to the living rooms. Only through endless repetition of the burning process and trying to do different things with the furnace did I discover at some point that behind the stove there was a small lever which had to be turned to the right, so that the heat will remain in the oven and will not evaporate. Because of this small change, I was not only able to keep the living areas at a comfortable temperature, but also made around € 5000 of annual savings in heating costs. Only a few inches had decided whether I needed to spend € 5000 more or less per year in heating costs and whether it was 15 degrees more or less over a total area of 2000 m^2!

Such a small change had such huge consequences (butterfly effect)!

And these are just the immediate and obvious results. It was not possible to predict the knock-on effects of this small change. Maybe my guests feel more comfortable in the apartments now because it's warmer and perhaps they recommend the apartments more often to their friends. Maybe I could use the € 5000 per year that I am now saving, to complete the refurbishment of the other new apartments faster. It could result in more events being held in the events hall or longer conferences than before, therefore bringing people together who might later change the world. It is simply not possible to predict the immense impact that a small lever could have.

Resistance of belief

Although Galileo Galilei had insisted that the sun does not revolve around the earth, but rather vice versa, and even though they ostracized him for this, put him under arrest and wanted to kill him, a large proportion of the general population believed for many decades and centuries (!) that the earth was the center of the universe. The church, as well as almost everyone else who recognized the church, believed this as well. Why should it be any different?

It was not until 1992 (!), approximately 350 years after Galileo's[xv] death, that the Catholic church officially rehabilitated him.

The general public does not think critically, but accepts general thinking without analyzing it.

The world actually holds dreamers back from doing something good in it, simply because much of what dreamers want to do does not fit into the common worldview. Of course, this resistance can be stifling for dreamers. The more of this resistance they feel, the more distant they perceive the prospect of their dreams actually coming true.

General belief and general opinion lead us to believe that our actions have no impact or only quite a minor impact. Our self-confidence is often dented. We are supposed to blend in with the crowd and to believe that we are nothing more than a number in society. It makes us believe that we, and everything we do, do not matter. The world really wants us to believe this!

If you begin to believe that you are important and relevant, your actions will also be relevant.

The truth is that even the smallest movement has eternal consequences and therefore it is worth taking action.

Pavlov Effect

Most give up when they see hurdles. If they cannot break through or overcome hurdles after 3 attempts, the Pavlov principle automatically kicks in.

Many years ago, the Russian physician and physiologist Ivan Pavlov[xvi] studied this phenomenon of conditioning.

If you show a piece of meat to a dog and each time he comes towards the meat, the dog gets a light smack on the head instead of the meat, it will not come the fourth time you show him the meat.

It also works the other way around. If you give a piece of meat to the dog every time you ring a bell, eventually the dog will come when he hears the bell, although there is no meat.

There is a conditioning process taking place here. In humans, this conditioning can take place if we suffer frequent rejection or cannot overcome hurdles. However, this conditioning is purely psychological and has nothing to do with reality! Maybe it would prove to be lucky the fourth time.

Anyone who has ever been trapped in the Pavlov principle no longer believes in the leverage effect, the butterfly effect, and in his own dreams. The system is designed in such a way that we lose faith. However, if we keep in mind that everything we do will have eternal consequences, then we break through the wall of resistance. However, this is only possible with the help of the heart and firm convictions. However, most lose their faith against the wall of resistance.

The dream autopilot

In the chapter on "repeating" we have learned that repetition can give us a decisive advantage: the opportunity to fix mistakes and to make minor adjustments. Repetition is very important for a completely different reason, because repetition strengthens the belief in our own goal and makes us aware that we are able to achieve our goals.

At the beginning of a project, a process of change or training, many people are very upbeat and confident. They have a firm belief in their dreams and goals!

At some point however, they realize that they are not progressing as quickly as they had thought and that success does not come as rapidly as they would wish. Many of them neglect their training and they gradually lose faith in their goal. They do not believe in their dream any longer and the motivation curve falls sharply. They quickly look for secondary goals.

If the dreamer cannot bring himself to take the training again and to regain a little belief, he should not be surprised if he remains stuck at the same level and starts to gain satisfaction through achieving lesser targets. However, should the dreamer begin his repetition again, he will quickly regain confidence and will have renewed faith that he is on the right track.

Repetition restores our faith!

Switch to autopilot! When you have repeated something often enough, the body and mind get used to the situation which now becomes a new state of well-being. We switch the autopilot on. This state of well-being is now the norm. It is the perfect base from which to compete and to reach new heights.

Why is this so?

Basically, because our brains works that way. Most of all, it turns the autopilot on, because our normal environment means routines and habitual activities. Our brain does not have to adapt to anything new and can run pretty smoothly. If you repeat something often enough, you will eventually switch to autopilot. The repetitive state becomes the new norm.

People who make it a habit to get up at a certain time, to always shave, to look in the mirror, to make coffee, people who perform these steps again and again in this semi-conscious state, buttoning a shirt, drinking coffee without thinking critically, is in a state of well-being. Everything is running like clockwork, as if you are on autopilot. This is the state in which we feel most comfortable and this is achieved with repetition. That's why repetition is important.

If you repeatedly hop on one leg to go to work, at some stage you will switch to this state of well-being and it will become normal. Getting into the habit of swimming 10 laps in the swimming pool every day will similarly give you this feeling of well-being. It is also called the flow state.

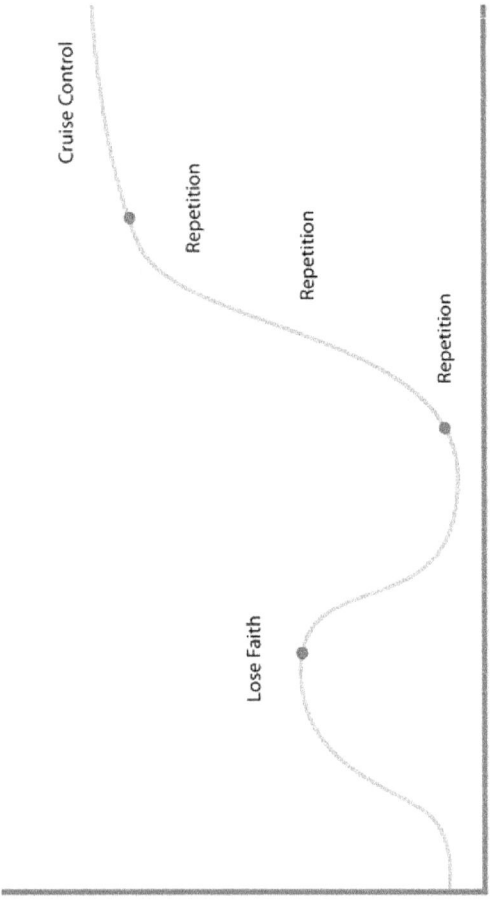

Chaos Theory

Chaos theory is one of the fundamental principles upon which our world, and even the whole universe, works.

Chaos theory suggests that order can always be found, even in chaos. A hurricane seems to be quite chaotic and destructive, but even a hurricane follows a certain pattern.

Dreamers who want to change the world, who want to be geniuses and want to tear down long-standing walls, must apply the principle of the hurricane. Especially in the beginning, anything new, innovative and creative threatens the established structures in our society. Creative thinking creates chaos, which is why it is often mocked and new ideas are belittled.

But all the order in our world was initially created from chaos. This is an irrefutable principle that we must not forget. The dreamer brings his creative clutter to the existing order. This creates something new! Inertia is replaced by progress.

It is important to allow new innovations to take root. Even with such basic disciplines as agriculture, this is vital. Even if my warehouse is full of wheat, at some point it will run out and by then we will all have starved. Only if we grow new wheat will we have enough.

We humans tend to want to rest on our laurels. This is also the reason why many people do everything possible to maintain the status quo. But the wheat stocks are limited and running out! We live off dreams, new life. Even a single grain can turn into a whole field.

Even an apple contains many cores, each of which contains two other cores. If you plant these seeds to grow a tree, it creates unlimited possibilities. Hundreds or even thousands of trees grow over a period of years from a single apple tree, but if you only try to live off the supply of apples in the cellar, the stockpile will eventually be exhausted. Therefore, the entire global economy and culture needs chaotic, creative, brainstorming thinkers and visionaries to create new life! We cannot live off the stockpile forever.

So don't worry if things look chaotic at first! Chaos has always been the beginning of something big.

Renaissance 3.0

Like everything in the world, this book of course is also based on the principle of the butterfly effect. In this world there are countless people who have serious dreams but who might not know how they can realize their dreams, or simply are not confident enough and only require the decisive push.

Let us imagine that this book helps only 5% of these dreamers to turn their dreams into reality. What impact might this have on our planet?

A New Renaissance

Many people today recognize the Renaissance as a period of European history characterized mainly by works of art, architecture and music, but the real starting point for it lay elsewhere.

After the fall of the Roman Empire, the continent fell gradually into the less enlightened Middle Ages. The aristocracy and the church were particularly powerful, and created an atmosphere in which progress was scarcely allowed to flourish. Individuals and their talents were not held in high regard.

It was not until the 14th and 15th centuries that a general "awakening" began to emerge, through which people no longer viewed their circumstances as a given fact. Even works from ancient Rome, Greece and the Arab world were rediscovered and brought knowledge with them. In addition to purely religious views, more and more secular and open perspectives began to establish themselves.

This development, which first took place in the minds of the people, basically paved the way for many developments and inventions in all fields, which changed society, arts, politics and even the economy. The Renaissance, the time of "awakening," paved the way for some European countries to become economic, military and political world powers and to kick start centuries of progress.

The Renaissance 3.0

In many ways, we can see a similar situation today. Although the church and its power have faded into relative insignificance, most people today still hold the view that their actions have little effect and they cannot create change. There is an obsessive, compulsive thinking that has little to do with reality and sometimes even an outright lack of direction or inability to change.

What is needed is a new awakening, a new self-confidence and perhaps even a Renaissance 3.0.

If people today didn't just run dreams through their heads, but also had the courage and confidence to strike out and to act differently in order to make a difference, it might be possible not only to solve the problems of this world, but perhaps even achieve the common dreams of mankind.

We should not forget that our every action has consequences and sometimes powerful tools in them that we should use.

Whether you cheat the system or not, everything has an effect. You can evade your taxes, albeit only 50 euros, but if everyone paid this 50 euros and everyone complied with the rules, the entire system would inevitably change. It cannot be otherwise!

Examples like this can be found everywhere. Nowadays, it takes ten policemen to patrol just a few blocks for illegal parking. But of what benefit is it to society if a cop goes up and down the road issuing tickets for illegal parking? Is that not a waste of time and energy for society? And last but not least, a financial drain? In Central Europe it probably costs around 2000–3000 euros per month to employ a policeman. Multiplied by ten policemen and one year, 10 years, 20 years, you end up with huge sums. In the end, tickets would still be issued for illegal parking. Instead, the policeman could also do something more meaningful to ensure safety and order. Could we not use our energies more wisely? If everyone just does one small good deed and parks his car properly, this will change the system!

Whether it relates to corruption or other areas, when people are aware that the behavior of an individual can have a tremendous impact on society and the entire world and this awareness is translated into action, it will change the world.

It is a universal truth, but the current system prevents us from believing it.

If we succeed in enabling only 5% of the dreamers of the world to realize their dreams, this will have an impact on the remaining 95%. During the Renaissance, dreamers made the change. Let's say goodbye to compulsive thinking and let's start to act differently! Let's start behaving differently.

Let's start the Renaissance 3.0 now

"I really do inhabit a system in which words are capable of shaking the entire structure of government, where words can prove mightier than ten military divisions."

Vaclav Havel

Little hinges swing big doors!

Starting over three times

In my life I have changed course three times and started over again three times and re-invented myself completely. Of course, I still have a lot to do and it may well be that I will have to reinvent myself once again or several times more in my life. I am convinced that anyone can do it if he only accepts some of the advice in this book with open eyes and ears.

As mentioned, our world needs dreamers more than ever. Now is the time for these dreamers to have confidence and to speak out about their dreams, rather than allowing them to drift, eventually realizing when it is too late that so much time and so many chances have been lost.

Did you find your missing link?

Each person is unique, has his or her own experiences and backgrounds and also his own dreams. Therefore, there is no timetable for dreams that can be applied 100% to every dream, but there are some basic rules and mechanisms that have endured in our world for thousands of years that can be helpful in making a dream reality.

It is therefore not essential to implement all the suggestions in this book immediately, one after the other. It is important that everyone has found the help they need for their lives and for their dreams. Maybe only a tiny push is needed to finally realize a dream, perhaps from this book. A dream is like a puzzle and if only one piece of the puzzle is missing, the picture cannot be completed. Sometimes it is enough just to take a step to the left or right to put yourself in the right place! I am convinced that the readers of this book are on the right track. Your interest in this book alone clearly demonstrates humility before the world and that you have the courage to ask for help.

It must never be forgotten that a change in personality is needed to achieve great things and great things can also be very simple. Everyone is entitled to his own dream and to shout it out loud. Believe in the unstoppable momentum of those who are beginning a new chapter (serendipity).

Flumina de ventre eius fluent aquae vivae: *The power to achieve our dreams is inside all of us!*

Butterfly Effect on Dreams: *The flapping of a butterfly's wings in Japan triggers a hurricane in South America.*

If you will it, it is no longer a dream: *Once the switch is turned on in the mind, it becomes reality!*

3Ds: Without deeds, dreams are dead. Deeds make our dreams dance.

Redwood principle: *If you aim high, you have to put down strong roots (in the heart).*

Domino Effect: *Any small action can have countless major effects.*

Ask, Pursue, Act: *He who asks, shows humility!*

Whatever you can do, or dream you can do, begin it: *Take the first step and help is sure to come.*

Archimedes: Give me a lever long enough and a fulcrum on which to place it, and I shall move the world.

Metamorphosis: *He who wants to change his life, must be willing to change himself.*

Newton's 3rd Law: Every action has a reaction.

2000 years have become reality

VAT: *Often it is enough to add only a little value.*

KISS: *Keeping it simple and easy.*

Decision & Commitment: *As soon as someone is definitely committed to his cause, fate takes its course!*

Metamorphosis contra Agere: *Fear must become self-awareness.*

Chaos Theory: *Wherever there is order, there is disorder. Disorder is the basis for new life!*

H-H-H: *From head to heart to hands*

About the author:

Raja Oellinger-Guptara is a changemaker creating and supporting sustainability projects. His aim is to develop strategies for combining the uniqueness of the past with the needs of the future and to convey the necessity to distinguish between what is important and what is essential. "We have the power to change any moment, at any time."

He is involved in many tourist projects, including Geinberg Suites, ViaNova Center and Bäckerbergerhof. Raja studied around the world, from New Delhi to Miami. He is a founder and investor of Kingscurry AG, currently the single largest chain of Indian restaurants in continental Europe.

http://www.youtube.com/watch?v=rC60en_vgmY

Note of thanks

My special thanks to serendii publishing, without which this book would not have been possible.

"Thanks to all who wish to have a different, better world"

Raja Öllinger-Guptara

Further support concerning dreams:

More information about "The Midas Effect," as well as important information about the realization of dreams, can be found at the following links:

www.the-midas-effect.com

www.facebook.com/midaseffect

All readers will also receive a 20% discount on the Changemaker seminars at Geinberg Suites in Geinberg, Austria with Raja Öllinger-Guptara.

To receive the discount, simply find the first word in the chapter, "Metamorphosis contra agere" in the text and send it to office@geinberg-suites.com.

Index

_____

[i] http://en.wikipedia.org/wiki/Butterfly_effect 17.02.2014
[ii] www.hargassner.at
[iii] Paulo Coelho, The Alchemist, ISBN 978-0061233845
[iv] Theodor Herzl, The Jewish State, ISBN 978-0557152087
[v] Theodor Herzl, Old New Land, ISBN 978-1558761605
[vi] http://en.wikipedia.org/wiki/Mc_Donalds 17.02.2014
[vii] http://en.wikipedia.org/wiki/Serendipity 17.02.2014
[viii] Malcom Gladwell, The Tipping Point, ISBN 978-0316679077
[ix] Federico Pistono, Robots will steal your job, but that´s ok, ISBN 978-1479380008
[x] Liz Wiseman, Lois N. Allen, Elise Foster, The Multiplier Effect – Tapping the Genius inside our schools, ISBN 978-1452271897
[xi] Malcom Gladwell, Outliers: The Story of Success, ISBN 978-0316017930
[xii] http://www.nytimes.com/2007/01/03/nyregion/03life.html?_r=0 17.02.2014
[xiii] Malcom Gladwell, Blink – The power of thinking without thinking, ISBN 978-0316010665
[xiv] www.en.wikipedia.org/wiki/Fosbury_Flop 17.02.2014
[xv] http://en.wikipedia.org/wiki/Galileo_Galilei 17.02.2014
[xvi] http://en.wikipedia.org/wiki/Ivan_Pavlov 17.02.2014

www.ingramcontent.com/pod-product-compliance
Lightning Source LLC
LaVergne TN
LVHW051559080426
835510LV00020B/3054